DATE DUE

JUN 2 7 2015

BRODART, CO.   Cat. No. 23-221

THE UNEXPLAINED

STONEHENGE

BY SEAN McDANIEL

BELLWETHER MEDIA · MINNEAPOLIS, MN

Are you ready to take it to the extreme?
Torque books thrust you into the action-packed world
of sports, vehicles, mystery, and adventure. These books
may include dirt, smoke, fire, and dangerous stunts.
WARNING: read at your own risk.

3 1218 00471 1603

Library of Congress Cataloging-in-Publication Data

McDaniel, Sean.
 Stonehenge / by Sean McDaniel.
    p. cm. -- (Torque: the unexplained)
 Summary: "Engaging images accompany information about Stonehenge. The combination of high-interest subject matter and light text is intended for students in grades 3 through 7"--Provided by publisher.
 Includes bibliographical references and index.
 ISBN 978-1-60014-645-9 (hardcover : alk. paper)
 1. Stonehenge (England)--Juvenile literature. 2. Wiltshire (England)--Antiquities--Juvenile literature. 3. Megalithic monuments--England--Wiltshire--Juvenile literature. I. Title.
 DA142.M38 2012
 936.2'319--dc22

                              2011002256

This edition first published in 2012 by Bellwether Media, Inc.

Printed in the United States of America, North Mankato, MN.

080111   1187

CONTENTS

CHAPTER 1
AN ANCIENT MYSTERY

Imagine England about 4,500 years ago. Hundreds of workers are building a large structure on an open plain. They use stone tools to cut giant slabs of sandstone. Deer antlers help them dig around the stones.

The workers use ropes to drag the stones at least 25 miles (40 kilometers) across the plain. Wooden levers help them stand the giant stones upright. Finally, the workers lift more stones to lie on top of the upright stones.

The stones form a circle that still stands today. This circle and the surrounding area is called Stonehenge. How did **ancient** people use this **monument**? Why did they go to such great effort to build it?

In 1995, a group of builders used ancient tools to move and stand huge stone blocks. This helped them understand how Stonehenge was built.

HEAVY LIFTING

CHAPTER 2
WHAT IS STONEHENGE?

England

Stonehenge

Stonehenge is an ancient monument that stands in southern England. The stones and the large, circular ditch that surrounds them form a **henge**. The strange circle of stones has puzzled people for centuries.

Archaeologists know that Stonehenge was built
in stages. The stages were often hundreds of years apart.
A simple henge was built in the first stage. It had a circle
of small stones.

Huge stones called **sarsens** were added around 2500 BCE. Each sarsen weighed around 90,000 pounds (40,823 kilograms). Workers placed stones called **lintels** on top of the sarsens. The sarsens and lintels form the outer ring of Stonehenge.

Altar Stone

bluestones

More stones stand inside the outer ring. They include a circle of small **bluestones**. Sarsens and lintels form a horseshoe shape in the middle of that circle. Within the horseshoe lies a smaller horseshoe of bluestones. A large stone called the Altar Stone lies in the center.

Over the years, people took many stones from Stonehenge. Today, the monument has been restored and the stones are protected.

A LONG HAUL

The bluestones probably came from the Preseli Mountains. This mountain range is 240 miles (386 kilometers) away from the monument.

THE STONEHENGE COMPLEX

Stonehenge is the most famous of a series of
related structures in southern England.

Name

Bluehenge

Bush Barrow

Durrington Walls

Stonehenge Avenue

Stonehenge Course

Woodhenge

Description

This small circle of bluestones stood near Stonehenge thousands of years ago. Archaeologists believe that its bluestones may have been moved to Stonehenge around 2000 BCE.

This burial mound near Stonehenge contained a golden dagger and other valuable objects.

This is the largest henge in the world. It measures about 1,640 feet (500 meters) across. It lies 2 miles (3.2 kilometers) northeast of Stonehenge.

This ancient road connected Stonehenge to Bluehenge.

Wide, parallel ditches and banks form the Stonehenge Course. It measures 2 miles (3.2 kilometers) long.

This henge near Stonehenge featured a pattern of wooden posts. It may have also had standing stones.

CHAPTER 3
SEARCHING FOR ANSWERS

What purpose did Stonehenge serve? People have many **theories**. One theory is that ancient priests called Druids used it as a temple. Some claim that a Druid named Merlin was in charge of the project. Others have suggested that **aliens** told the ancient people to build it.

Another theory is that ceremonies may have been held at the monument. The bodies of rich and powerful people have been found buried at the site.

Today, many people think Stonehenge served as an ancient calendar. Some stones mark the spots where the sun rises and sets on the summer and winter **solstices**. Some people think Stonehenge was used to study **astronomy**. The monument could have helped ancient people predict **eclipses**.

In 1953, archaeologist Richard Atkinson noticed carvings in some of the stones at Stonehenge. One stone had a carving of a dagger in it. He also found four carvings of axes. The carvings are only visible when the sunlight hits them in the right spot.

SHEDDING SOME LIGHT

We know some facts about Stonehenge, but much remains a mystery. Will we ever know the true purpose of Stonehenge? Or does the monument hold deeper secrets that may never be revealed?

GLOSSARY

aliens—beings from other planets

ancient—existing more than 1,500 years ago

archaeologists—scientists who study ancient civilizations

astronomy—the study of space, including stars, planets, and moons

bluestones—small stones made from cooled lava that form the inner ring of Stonehenge

eclipses—events in which a planet or a moon blocks sunlight from reaching another planet or moon

henge—an ancient structure featuring a large, flat area surrounded by a circular ditch or dirt wall; the flat area often contains stone structures.

lintels—stones that rest horizontally on top of the sarsens at Stonehenge

monument—a structure that reminds people of an important person, event, or time period

sarsens—the large, upright stones of Stonehenge

solstices—the days of the year when the sun is at its northernmost or southernmost point; one solstice happens in the summer and the other happens in the winter.

theories—ideas that try to explain why something exists or happens

TO LEARN MORE

AT THE LIBRARY

Gray, Leon. *Solving the Mysteries of Stonehenge*. New York, N.Y.: Marshall Cavendish Benchmark, 2009.

Petrini, Catherine M. *Stonehenge*. Farmington Hills, Mich.: KidHaven Press, 2006.

Riggs, Kate. *Stonehenge*. Mankato, Minn.: Creative Education, 2009.

ON THE WEB

Learning more about Stonehenge is as easy as 1, 2, 3.

1. Go to www.factsurfer.com.

2. Enter "Stonehenge" into the search box.

3. Click the "Surf" button and you will see a list of related Web sites.

With factsurfer.com, finding more information

INDEX

The images in this book are reproduced through the courtesy of: Chris Knapton/Alamy, front cover, pp. 18-19; Markus Gann, p. 4; Mary Evans Picture Library/The Image Works, p. 5; Andrew Parker/Alamy, pp. 6-7; Jon Eppard, pp. 8, 16-17; Last Refuge/Photolibrary, p. 9; David Nunuk/ Photolibrary, pp. 10-11; Photolibrary, pp. 12-13; Liquid Productions, LLC, pp. 14-15; Brian Seed/Alamy, p. 18 (small); Juan Martinez, pp. 20-21.